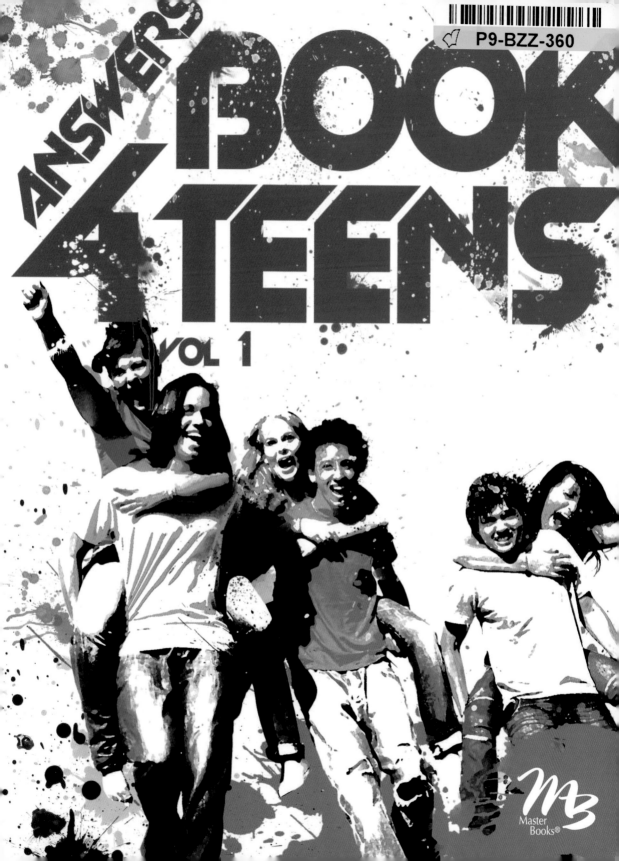

ANSWERS BOOK 4 TEENS

VOL 1

Master Books®

First printing: October 2011
Fourth printing: November 2014

ISBN: 978-0-89051-622-5
Library of Congress Number: 2011937097

Cover by Justin Skinner

Unless otherwise noted, Scripture quotations are from the New King James Version of the Bible.

Please consider requesting that a copy of this volume be purchased by your local library system.

Printed in China

Please visit our website for other great titles: www.masterbooks.net

For information regarding author interviews, please contact the publicity department at (870) 438-5288

Master Books®
A Division of New Leaf Publishing Group
www.masterbooks.net

Contents

INTRODUCTION

I've worked with teens for years ... and there is a big misconception about them (and hopefully you will agree) ... they are much smarter than we often think! The young people I've worked with are intelligent and bright.

Yeah, I'll admit, some are smarter in some areas than others; in other words, some may know a lot about music, others know a lot about science, others know a lot of sports, and so on, but the point is they are much brighter than many people give them credit for. So with this book series, we are not going to be afraid to answer the questions they have without a "bunch of fluff," but with solid biblical answers that "have some meat to them" and challenge the secular religions like atheism and evolution that are forced on them in many settings — like movies, schools, and so on.

To do this, I want to define some terms, people, and worldviews just to make sure we are on the same page as we jump into these questions:

- **Secular humanism** (secular, humanism, secularists) is a religion that teaches that man is the ultimate authority on all matters, not God. In fact, this religion says God does not exist and they say that there are no supernatural things, but only natural/material things. This is the only religion permitted to be taught as fact in the public schools.

- **Evolution** (molecules-to-man evolution) is part of the religion of secular humanism. There are four major aspects of evolution:

- **Astronomical evolution** that teaches matter and energy came from nothing — called the **big bang** where the universe supposedly created itself.

- **Geological evolution** teaches that rock layers represent millions of years of sedimentation. Secularists claim that the rock layers were laid down slowly and gradually in the past over millions of years without catastrophes — such as worldwide floods, earthquakes, volcanic eruptions, etc.

- **Chemical evolution** that teaches that life came from non-life when chemicals supposedly came together to form the first life.

- **Biological evolution** that teaches that this first life evolved to be more complex through mutations and natural selection over millions of years to arrive at what we have today.

- **Natural selection** is a process described by a Christian named Ed Blyth about 25 years before Darwin to explain variations within created kinds (variations within dogs for example). Darwin thought this process could lead to evolution — most evolutionists today disagree with Darwin as they recognize this process loses information and is moving in the wrong direction for evolution! So now they appeal to mutations as the main mechanism.

- **Mutations** are changes in your DNA (*deoxyribonucleic acid,* which is the information building blocks for you and me) — like copying mistakes. Many have no effects, but others cause major problems like cancer or deformities. But evolutionists really hope that mutations used to cause changes to help us evolve from single-celled organisms to humans. But in reality, they are moving in the wrong direction for evolution as well.

- **Jesus Christ** is the Creator (John 1, Colossians 1, Hebrews 1), the second person of the one triune God (another word for trinity; consisting of God the Father, Christ, and the Holy Spirit) — God who stepped into history to become a man and die to sins on our behalf. Through Christ alone came salvation from sin and death.

- **Trinity** is the term we use to describe God because of His attributes and persons in the Bible. It is one God but three persons (Father, Son, and Holy Spirit). Analogies are never perfect but the one church fathers used was an equilateral triangle. It has three identical points but they are different points. Yet it is one triangle where each line of each angle is what makes up the lines of the other angles!

- **Biblical Christianity** is religion that is based on God being the ultimate authority and His Word, the Bible, dictates the basis for all things.

- **The Bible** is the written Word of God given to the Jews by the prophets of the Old Testament and on the Church by the Apostles of the New Testament. There are 66 books of the Bible —— 39 in the Old Testament and 27 in the New Testament.

- **Atheism** is a variant form of humanism that says **THERE IS NO GOD.** (So apparently people who say this think they have looked everywhere in the natural and supernatural world at exactly the same time to make this claim! Yeah, right!)

- **Agnosticism** is a variant form of humanism that says **IT IS IMPOSSIBLE TO KNOW** if there is a God. (But, of course, how can they know that!)

- **Creationists** are people who believe the Bible to be the absolute authority in all areas including origins. They are biblical Christians who believe in creation as described in the Bible including the biblical age of the earth, the literal fall of mankind, and a global Flood.

- **Created kinds:** the Bible speaks of animal kinds. These are not exactly the same as species, but instead can be explained by descriptions like a horse kind or a dog kind. Within a kind you may have different animals — for example, a donkey and a zebra are within the horse kind, and being part of the same kind, they can reproduce to create a zonkey. (*He's kinda cute, isn't he!*)

Any other terms we use, we hope to discuss in the context of the book, but we wanted to make sure we were on the same page as we began.

Now teens . . . let's get started.

Bodie Hodge, *Answers in Genesis*

How can anyone believe that the Bible is true since it was written so long ago when

PEOPLE DIDN'T KNOW STUFF?

Bodie Hodge

PEOPLE DIDN'T KNOW STUFF?

Well . . . the first thing that needs to be addressed is the false issue of "people not knowing stuff." This is an evolutionary assumption. In the evolutionary story, people evolved from ape-like creatures and they were "dumb brutes" that slowly got smarter.

According to the Bible, God made Adam and Eve perfectly! In fact, they were "programmed" with perfect knowledge, and they could talk to God right from the start! So people were indeed smart and knew stuff right from the start — cool, huh?

GOOD ANSWERS OFFERING NO PROOF

Many well-meaning Christians have put forth a number of arguments for the Bible to be true. Most of these arguments are not the best ones to use. They are sometimes a good confirmation that the Bible is true, but not proof of it. I'll summarize some of these here.

• **The Bible says it is the Word of God, hence the truth because God is the truth.**
If Johnny Smith writes an essay and says it is the Word of God does that make it so? Nope. But it is good the Bible makes the claim of being the Word of God, because if it didn't, there would be no reason to think it is the Word of God!

• **Variations of cool Bible facts and uniqueness of the Bible.** Definitely unique: written over the course of about 2,000 years with over 40 authors, including a shepherd and a king, is scientifically, archaeologically, and historically accurate, with no errors, prophetically 100 percent, one theme centered around the Fall of mankind and salvation through Christ, and even the last two chapters of the Bible undo what happened in the third chapter of the Bible! But this still isn't proof of truthfulness of the Bible. Though, we expect the Bible to be all these things, they are still not proof.

Let's look at the correct answer in some more detail.

IMAGE OF GOD

When God created man, He made us in His image, unlike plants and animals. Think of this for a moment — we are made in the image of a truthful, logical, loving God! This is why we care, why we can think logically, and why we have an understanding of what truth is. This is why we can ask the question "is the Bible true?" and why we can think "logically" about it — squirrels have never asked me if the Bible were true after all!

See, if the Bible weren't true — we would have no basis for truth to even exist. Or for that matter we would have no basis for logic to exist. In fact, we would have no basis for knowledge at all! There would be no reason for clothes, weekends, marriage, love, science, literature, and so on. Wow! Never thought about the Bible that way, have you?

SO HOW DO WE KNOW THE BIBLE IS TRUE?

Answer: It has to be; all other worldviews fall short and make knowledge impossible, except the Bible. The Bible is the only book that has the basis for knowledge and logic (in other words, only the Bible has necessary foundational knowledge that makes intelligence possible).

All other worldviews (Islam, Hinduism, Mormonism, Atheism, Agnosticism, etc.) must borrow from the Bible to make sense of things. Science, morality, and logic all stem from the Bible being true. So to repeat, if the Bible were not true, then knowledge would be impossible. In other words, if the Bible were not true, nothing would make sense — good or bad — everything would be meaningless and pointless.

Yeah, it seems complicated, right, but don't let it scare you! **Here's an example:**

One day I was called to deal with an evolutionary atheist who was questioning a young Christian lady. As I approached, the atheist was firing off question after question to the lady and not even permitting her to respond. Every time she tried, he would ask another question with a rather aggressive tone.

When I entered into the conversation the skeptic turned to me and then, he went into a tirade of questions attacking Christianity one question after another . . . with me. Every time I tried to respond, he cut me off with another question.

I realized that he obviously didn't believe the Bible and that was one of the main issues, besides the fact that he didn't want to hear a response. While he was taking a breath, I slipped in a question that silenced him. I asked him, "Why are you wearing clothes?" He was shocked speechless. So I asked again and then said something to the effect that "animals don't get up in the morning and put clothes on." I continued by saying, "You are an atheist, right, where you believe people are just animals, so why are you wearing clothes?"

Then he paused and thought for a moment and said, "Because it's cold." So I instantly came back and said, "When it warms up you don't wear clothes?" Obviously, he had not considered, in his professed worldview, why he wore clothes, yet there he was, with shirt and pants on!

9

I explained that he wears clothes because in a literal Genesis, a literal Adam and a literal Eve ate a literal fruit and literally disobeyed God and that caused us to be literally shameful. God killed an animal and clothed Adam and Eve. So we wear clothes as a result. And in your heart of hearts, you know God exists and the Bible is true, as your actions reveal that you know you are shameful (Romans 1).

Then I noticed he was wearing a wedding ring. So I asked, "Why did you get married?" He said because he loved his wife. I pointed out that love, in an atheistic worldview is no different from sadness, both being chemical reactions in the brain that are essentially meaningless (yep . . . that is what atheists really believe!). Love exists in a Christian worldview where we are made in the image of a loving God.

I also pointed out that getting married is contrary to what atheists would teach. You have one basic goal in an atheistic evolutionary story: to pass on your genes to as many people as you can. Getting married and being faithful to one woman (which he said he was and we need to understand is the only biblical teaching on marriage, by the way) is going against what an evolutionary atheist professes should be going on. I continued by saying that marriage comes from the Bible, specifically in Genesis, because God created a literal man and a literal woman, hence the first marriage.

After all this, the atheist just stopped to think about what we had discussed (obviously not wanting to believe it). His hostile tone was gone and he realized that he didn't have answers to defend his atheistic worldview.

What I needed to do was show him that even though he claimed to be an atheist and evolutionist, he had no basis in his religion to wear clothes or get married. Those things come from the Bible being true! So I needed to show him where he was borrowing from the Bible. It just goes to reveal how people know the Bible's true in their hearts (Romans 2:15) and inadvertently live their lives according to it many times, yet in their own religions say they don't believe it is true. They must borrow from the Bible even to argue against it!

Why Is This So Important?

Well, it should be obvious that if the Bible were not true, nothing would matter and nothing would make sense: friends, love, morality . . . nothing. Sadly, many kids today are taught that the Bible is not true, and they begin to live their lives like this . . . don't they? And we can see the terrible effects of it all around us.

If God's really so great, why does He let so much pain and bad stuff happen in the world, like

EARTHQUAKES, FLOODS, AND WARS?

Dr. Tommy Mitchell

The "bad" things that occur in our world — earthquakes, floods, wars —are ultimately the result of our sin. Natural disasters and such are really just a small taste of what life is like apart from God. They remind us that the consequences of sin are very serious.

In the beginning, God created a world that He, Himself, called "very good" (Genesis 1:31). **Here there was no death, no suffering, no pain.** It was Adam's disobedience that brought death and corruption to this "very good" creation. By his actions, Adam was saying, in effect, "God, I don't like Your rules. I want to live the way I want to live." Adam had the option to obey or disobey God. He obviously chose poorly. The world has felt the effects of that choice since that day.

God is the righteous judge of all the earth (Psalm 9:8, Psalm 50:6). Genesis 18:25 testifies, "Shall not the Judge of all the earth do right?" Because He is just, He must punish sin. God judged Adam's sin. The punishment was death — Adam forfeited the right to live. The perfect creation was cursed since Adam and Eve had dominion. The whole dominion fell when they fell (Genesis 3; Romans 8:22). This all took place because of man's rebellion — sin.

It's true that God is all-powerful (Job 42:2). He is in control of His creation. He is the Creator of the land, the sea, and the universe, and the wind and the waves obey Him (Matthew 8:23–27). But because He is also the Judge of all creation, He cannot overlook sin. To do so would be against His character, and God cannot act contrary to His character.

Sadly, we do have wars, which are the result of people who aren't able to get along. We see sickness and disease. We see children dying. There are disasters, like earthquakes and tsunamis. If God is love, then why do these things happen? **Again the answer is, it's OUR fault.** So we need to stop blaming God for the way the world is and acknowledge that it is because of our sin. **Who broke this world? We did!**

We, through Adam, separated ourselves from our God. And we would be separated forever (even though our bodies die, because we are made in the image of God, our souls live forever) — but God had a plan to rescue us from the effects of sin and its eternal consequence of separation from God. He stepped into history in the person of His Son, Jesus Christ, to pay the penalty for sin (death) by dying on a Cross. **He rose from the dead** (meaning He has ultimate power, as He conquered death), and **offers a free gift of salvation to all who will receive it.**

Now while God could prevent bad things from happening in this world, we can trust that because He is good, He has good reasons for allowing bad things to happen (even if we as finite beings cannot not always understand it). He is working things for good, and we pray He receives the glory (Romans 8:28). One of the most important examples of this is the death of Jesus on the Cross (John 3:16). This was an evil event, yet God used it to bring salvation to all of us if we receive it.

Let's think of this question in another way. **Because God is good, He defines what is good and bad**. So only those who believe in God and His Word are able to declare one event "good" (for example, the curing of a disease or the birth of a baby) and another event "bad" (for example, a tsunami that destroys human life).

If there is no God, who or what is our basis for determining good and bad? I am. You are. We would each then determine what is right or wrong — imagine a world like that! Those who don't believe in God don't have any way to absolutely say that one thing is good and another thing is bad.

So when we ask questions that deal with things that are bad, we need to make sure that we're accepting God's standards for good and bad and not making up our own set of rules. (It's tempting to think it would be more fun if we just could set our own rules for study hall and life, but what a mess we'd make of everything! Rules are around for a reason.)

When we hear of tragedies in any form, (remembering it is our fault — because of sin — these things happen), **we can look for ways to help others** — by donating needed items or money, or perhaps even working as a volunteer in a time of disaster or emergency. Most importantly, however, we need to pray and ask the Lord to help those who are hurting. We must pray that those who are suffering will, in their time of trial or difficulty, turn toward God and not away from Him. God wants to save us from what our sin did. It is in these difficult times that people need the peace that only God can provide (Philippians 4:7). **They must understand that He is the true source of comfort in a fallen and cursed world.**

I believe God created the earth, but does it really matter

HOW OLD THE EARTH IS?

Bodie Hodge

Yes, It Matters and Here's Why

The Bible teaches that God created all things in six normal-length days (the earth was created on day 1) and this is the basis for our work week (Exodus 20:11; Exodus 31:17). When Moses, inspired by the Holy Spirit, pointed this out in Exodus, the Israelites understood them as normal-length days (24 hours each) — they didn't work for a million years and rest for a million years! In fact, few Christians questioned the length of the days of creation (supposedly being millions of years long) until recent times. Even the phrases used in Genesis 1 (for example, "one day," "evening and morning," and so on) plainly reveal that each day was about 24 hours long. Days don't represent periods of millions of years. (Can you imagine a school day that lasted a million years? Chemistry already feels like forever!)

From carefully studying the ages given in the family tree lists (like those genealogical "father begat son" lists, in Genesis 5 and 11) and other ranges of time (for example, the period the Israelites were in Egypt and the length of time the kings of Israel and Judah reigned), we can tell that the length of time **from Adam until Jesus came to earth was about 4,000 years.**

The Bible itself doesn't leave room for the universe and earth to be much older than about 6,000 years. **Since the Bible is God's Word and God cannot lie** (Titus 1:2), **we trust what it teaches about the age of the earth**. This has nothing to do with whether you are saved or not. That is a matter of faith in Jesus Christ. The age of the earth matters because you either trust God or you don't. Many people trust God when He speaks of salvation, but not when He speaks on Genesis. And that makes no sense. We believe what God says about salvation and eternity, but don't want to believe what He says about how the world and all of us began.

WHAT'S GOING ON?

The idea of an old earth is part of the religion of secular humanism. These secularists reject God and His Word and claim fossil-containing rock layers were laid down slowly over millions of years. That is where the idea of an old earth comes from. But the Flood of Noah's day is what accounts for most of the rock layers that contain fossils (we've had some local floods, volcanoes, etc., that have made some layers since then). So we use the same evidence, but have a different interpretation due to different starting points (starting with the revelation from God in His Word, or starting with the ideas of man who was not there to see these layers being formed).

What is happening is that many Christians today do not trust God regarding Genesis. Instead, they trust imperfect, human speculations about the past, and sadly, they buy into the idea of an old earth. They are taking ideas from another religion and trying to mix it with the Bible. Some people "pick and choose" the parts of Christianity they want to believe and then mix it with aspects of secular humanism. With this, who is really the authority they are following: God or man?

When they take millions of years (geological evolution or big bang [astronomical evolution] and other evolutionary ideas) and mix it with the Bible, they can't fit it in the genealogies from Adam to Christ. So they try to put all the millions of years in Genesis 1. **But this causes a major problem!**

DEATH BEFORE SIN?

The age of the earth matters because of another important Bible truth. When God created the world, He declared it to be very good and perfect (Genesis 1:31; Deuteronomy 32:4). The plants He created on day 3 provided food for all living things (Genesis 1:29–30).

This changed when Adam disobeyed God's command about the Tree of the Knowledge of Good and Evil (this is the name of the tree they were told not eat from) (Genesis 2:16–17). God punished Adam and Eve for their sin, and that sin affected all of us. We are sinners living in a sin-cursed world as a result, and the punishment for sin is death (Genesis 3; Romans 5:12, 6:23). This is why we are all going to die sometime — because of sin.

The death we see all around us came about as a result of Adam's disobedience. Death had no place in God's original creation. No animal or human suffered from the emotional and physical pain of diseases such as cancer. No plants had thorns. No dinosaurs made a meal out of other creatures.

Yet the fossil record is full of this death and suffering — dead animals, bones showing evidence of cancer, plants with thorns, animals eating other animals, and so on. If the fossil record (and the earth in general) represents millions of years of suffering and death, then death and disease were part of God's creation long before humans came on the scene.

Death would no longer be the ultimate penalty for the sin of mankind but would be part of God's "very good" creation. But the Bible clearly lets us know death was not part of the perfect world. God describes death as an enemy: The last enemy that will be destroyed is death (1 Corinthians 15:26). Death is the result, or the punishment for sin. So death could not have been around for millions of years before sin (nor could the thorns, which also came about as a result of the curse in Genesis 3:18). This would undermine the entire reason that Christ came to save us from sin and death!

There is no way one can fit millions of years of death, disease, thorns, and animals eating animals into a "very good" creation where the animals (and humans) were vegetarian (Genesis 1:20-30). Such a "groaning" world had to come after sin (Romans 8:28). If rock layers formed in the Flood of Noah then we expect to find death, suffering, and thorns in the fossil layers.

Science and the Age of the Earth

Although it may seem as if secular scientists have "proven" the earth is millions of years old, this simply isn't true. In fact, the majority of the methods used to calculate estimates for the age of the earth give ages far less than millions or billions of years. The science is actually consistent with the Bible's age.

For example, scientific experiments have shown that coal can form under the right temperature and pressure in just a few weeks — not millions of years as is commonly taught.

Also, the moon is slowly spiraling away from earth. If the earth-moon system were really 4 billion years old, the moon would have been touching earth less than 1.5 billion years ago. But just 6,000 years ago, the moon would have been only 800 feet closer to earth, which makes much more sense.

Does the age of the earth matter? **Absolutely.** God's Word needs to be our final authority in every area it touches on (that is everything!). It clearly teaches that God created all things in six days about 6,000 years ago. Everything else is opinion — perhaps opinions by some professionals with lots of important-sounding degrees — but they are still opinions based on assumptions. These opinions seem to change every year anyway, unlike God, who knows everything and who always gets it right!

04

Who has the most evidence —

CREATIONISTS OR EVOLUTIONISTS?

Ken Ham

WE HAVE THE SAME EVIDENCE!

Sadly, the majority of Christians probably believe that the "evidence" overwhelmingly supports an old (millions of years) earth. But even those who keenly support Genesis still tend to see it as if there is a "mountain" of "their" facts/evidences lined up "against our side." For many, sadly, it causes them to reject what the Bible makes so plain about history, to the great detriment of the Gospel founded on that history.

Both of the above groups suffer from the same basic problem. They really don't understand that it is not a matter of "their evidence versus ours." All evidence is actually interpreted, and all scientists, in principle, actually have the same data available to them.

The background contains scattered handwritten equations:

$$L = -\frac{R}{L} \pm \sqrt{\left(\frac{R}{L}\right)^2 - 9}$$

$$u_c = U\left(1 - e^{-t/RC}\right)$$

$$C + O_2 \rightarrow CO_2$$

$$\frac{1}{TLC}$$

$$\omega = 2\pi f_r$$

$$4 FeS_2 + 11 O_2 \rightarrow 2 Fe_2 O_3 + 8 SO_2$$

$$?x \, \# y_i \quad ?=x$$

$$B \, dA = \oint E' \, dl = -\int_A \left(\frac{\partial B}{\partial t} + rot\,(B \times v)\right) dA$$

$$\rightarrow W_{rot} = \frac{1}{2} \cdot J\omega^2$$

$$a^2 = b^2 + c^2$$

$$H_2O \rightleftharpoons Cl^- + H_3O^+$$

$$\pi h \left(3e_1^2 + 3e_2^2 + L^2\right)$$

$$P_v = \int_{P=0}^{2\pi} \int_{\theta=0}^{\pi} \frac{r^2}{8 G_2} \, H_p \, H_p'' \sin\vartheta \, d\vartheta \, d\varphi$$

THE FACTS

I have often debated with evolutionists, or Christians who believe in evolution/millions of years, on various radio programs. Sometimes the interviewer has made statements like, *"Well, today we have a creationist who believes he has evidence for creation, and on the other side is an evolutionist who believes he has evidence to support evolution."*

I then stop the interviewer and state, *"I want to get something straight here. I actually have the same evidence the evolutionist has — the battle is not about the evidence or facts, as they are all the same. We live on the same earth, in the same universe, with the same plants and animals, the same fossils. The facts are all the same."*

Then the evolutionist says, *"But you're here about the Bible — this is religion. As an evolutionist I'm involved in real science."*

I then respond, *"Actually, as a creationist, I have no problem with your observational science; it's the same science I understand and trust. This is the science that builds our technology. The argument is not about observational science or about facts — ultimately, the argument is about how you interpret the facts — and this depends upon your belief about history — which we call historical or origins science). The real difference is that we have different "histories" (accounts about what happened in the past), which we use to interpret the facts of the present."*

I then give an example. *"Let's consider the science of genetics and natural selection. Evolutionists believe in natural selection — and what they call natural selection is real observational science, as you observe it happening. Well, creationists also believe in what is described as natural selection. Evolutionists accept the science of genetics — well, so do creationists.*

"However, here is the difference: Evolutionists believe that, over millions of years, one kind of animal has changed into a totally different kind. However, creationists, based on the Bible's account of origins, believe that God created separate kinds of animals and plants to reproduce their own kind — therefore one kind will not turn into a totally different kind.

"Now this can be tested in the present. The scientific observations support the creationist interpretation that the changes we see are not creating new information. The changes are all within the originally created pool of information of that kind; sorting, shuffling, or degrading it. The creationist account of history, based on the Bible, provides the correct basis to interpret the evidence of the present — and science of genetics confirms the interpretation."

My point is that if we Christians really understood that all evidence is actually interpreted on the basis of certain presuppositions, then we wouldn't be in the least bit intimidated by the evolutionists' supposed "evidence." Presuppositions are like a pair of glasses. You view the world through these sets of ideas or beliefs you had before you look at the facts. (Kind of like hating soy burgers before you bother to try one . . . or study one in science class!)

We should instead be looking at the evolutionist's (or old-earther's) interpretation of the evidence, and how the same evidence could be interpreted within a biblical framework and be confirmed by testable and repeatable science.

29

WHERE TO BEGIN

The bottom line is that it's not a matter of who has the better (or the most) "facts" on their side. The facts are the same — we simply interpret them differently by having a different starting point. So the next time evolutionists use what seem to be convincing facts for molecules to man (a.k.a. goo to you) evolution, try to determine the presuppositions they have used to interpret these facts.

Beginning with the big picture of history from the Bible, look at the same facts through these biblical glasses and interpret them differently. Then, using the same observational science in the present that an evolutionist also uses, see if that science, when properly understood, confirms (by being consistent with) the interpretation based on the Bible. **You will find over and over again that the Bible is confirmed by observational science.**

So let's not jump in a blind-faith way at the startling evidences we think we need to "prove" creation — trying to counter "their facts" with "our facts." (Jesus Himself rose from the dead in the most startling possible demonstration of the truth of God's Word. But still many wouldn't believe Luke 16:27–31.) Don't be intimidated by apparent "evidences" for evolution,

but understand the right way to think about evidence. We can then deal with the same evidence the evolutionists use, to show they have the wrong framework of interpretation — and that the facts of the real world really do conform to, and confirm, the Bible.

See? That is the only difference — our starting point for how we view history! Think of it like this: a person with a biblical worldview looks at you and sees a unique individual created by God; an evolutionist looks at you and sees a product of random accidents over countless generations. **You are still you** — it's just that people are "seeing" you differently! So when it comes down to it there are two different interpretations of the same data, but let's face it — both can't be right, and God is never wrong. In reality, all evidence is God's. So we expect to hear statements like:

Psalm 24:1 — The earth is the LORD'S, and all its fullness, The world and those who dwell therein.

With everything I hear about God not existing ...

HOW CAN WE EVEN KNOW THAT HE DOES EXIST?

Bodie Hodge

There are an increasing number of atheists out there, especially among teens. They have been taught this godless philosophy in schools by some peers, textbooks, and teachers (not all teachers . . . thank the Lord) that often mock God and say He doesn't exist. Many authors and editors of books, Internet sites, and movies also attack God and His character. Of course, they can't prove that God doesn't exist. But for some reason . . . if people hear something enough, they can be deceived into thinking it is true.

ATHEISM OFFERS NO EVIDENCE

So, to answer this question, let's first disprove atheism. I know this gets a bit philosophical (by that I mean ways of thinking, using logic and reason) — but when we talk about the existence of God and proving atheism wrong, we have to get a bit philosophical. But bear with me — this may be the toughest chapter in the whole book! But when you get it, you will get it!

I'm starting this way for a reason. Over ten years ago, I started a church class with teen guys for Bible study. The first thing we hit was a disproof of atheism . . . and they got excited because this was an answer they needed! They were tired of the "fluff" and they wanted some "meat."

33

Remember what atheists profess: There is no God. They are not saying "maybe there is a God" or "I don't know if there is a God"; **they are making the claim that God doesn't exist**! This is an absolute statement.

So one can ask the atheist . . . have you looked for God in the next room? Well, of course they haven't and if they had, you could also ask . . . did you look for God in St. Louis, Missouri, or some other city? Have they checked out at the moon, or in another galaxy? You could also asked how they "transcended" (went in to the spiritual realm) and looked for God there? God is spirit after all (John 4:24).

The point is, for them to say God does not exist, they must look everywhere in both the natural and supernatural realm at the exact same time to say God doesn't exist. Well, if you notice, they would have to be "all-knowing" (omniscient) and "everywhere" (omnipresent) to make such a claim. These are attributes of God! So the atheist who says, "There is no God" is claiming that he/she is God! Either way it refutes (disproves) the position of atheism! This is truly a foolish claim on their part (Psalm 14:1).

How Do We Know God Exists?

Christians have given a number of "philosophical" reasons for the existence of God.

Let's hit a few of these first.

1. **First Cause** (*everything seems to have a cause today, so if you go back far enough, to the first cause, it would be God*)

2. **Design** (*we see design everywhere in living things and so on, so there must be a Designer*)

3. **Ontological** (*tries to prove the existence of God by logical processes alone, e.g., logic being supreme to all*)

Each of these arguments for the existence of God uses logic and/or says logic exists and have certain characteristics: laws of logic don't change with time, apply everywhere, and so on. But how would laws of logic and their properties make sense in a godless universe? The fact that logic exists is the key to answering how we know God exists.

Dr. Jason Lisle of Answers in Genesis points out:

How could there be laws at all, without a law-giver? The atheist cannot account for (1) the existence of laws of logic, (2) why they are immaterial, (3) why they are universal, (4) why they do not change with time, (5) how human beings can possibly know about them or their properties. But of course, all these things make perfect sense in the Christian system.

Laws of logic owe their existence to the biblical God. Yet, they are required to reason rationally, to prove things. So, the biblical God must exist in order for reasoning to be possible. Therefore, the best proof of God's existence is that without Him we couldn't prove anything at all! The existence of the biblical God is the prerequisite for knowledge and rationality.

The best argument is that without God, we can't prove anything at all. No one could prove a thing. So, in trying to prove anything, God must exist! This is called the transcendental argument *(TAG)*, and these others (first cause, design, ontological) are actually inadvertently assuming it is true, just to attempt to make their claims! But this line of argumentation helps us step back and realize there is nothing greater than God (Hebrews 6:13). Isn't it fascinating that the Bible reveals of our Creator God (Jesus Christ):

"in whom are hidden all the treasures of wisdom and knowledge" (Colossians 2:3).

Q6

Come on, why would God punish the whole world for

ONE GUY'S MISTAKE?

Bodie Hodge

As we've seen in earlier questions, in the beginning, God said His creation of all things was "very good" (Genesis 1:31). **We expect nothing less from a perfect God!**

On the sixth day of the creation week, God made the first two people. Remember them? You got it — Adam and Eve. He gave Adam several responsibilities. Adam was to eat only plants and take care of the garden, for example. He was free to eat from any tree, except one — the Tree of the Knowledge of Good and Evil. It was a test of obedience. God warned Adam that if he disobeyed, he would surely die (Genesis 2:16–17). As the Creator, God is the One who sets the rules. And He determines the punishment for disobeying them.

It wasn't about the tree. It wasn't about the fruit. It was all about God giving Adam a rule and Adam choosing to break that rule. **Adam wasn't created like a puppet** — God wanted Adam to love and obey Him because he wanted to. So Adam was put to the test!

Eve was deceived by the serpent, which was influenced by Satan; that is why the serpent made sense in the first place — imagine if Satan influenced a parrot! She ate and Adam then ate the fruit from the Tree of the Knowledge of Good and Evil (Genesis 3:1–7). Adam didn't do it accidentally — he deliberately chose to rebel against his Creator. Disobeying God's commands is called sin. **Because God is holy, which means He is without sin, He cannot allow sin — any sin, even one — to go unpunished.**

Since He put Adam in charge of His creation and gave him the instruction not to eat that particular fruit, God held Adam responsible for what happened. Because of sin, God placed a curse on the serpent (Genesis 3:14), the animals (Genesis 3:14), and the ground (Genesis 3:17). Paul even reveals the extent of this in Romans 8:22 being the whole creation!

There were implications for the woman as well that included increased pain and sorrows (Genesis 3:16), and like Adam, sin resulted in death (Genesis 3:19–22). Sin affects more than just one person, huh? Absolutely. When a king or queen makes a bad decision for their kingdom, the whole kingdom suffers as a result. It was much like this. **The entire world was made to suffer the effects of sin.** This shows us how seriously God views sin. Because we, in Adam, sinned against God, we forfeited our right to live. We would have to die! Now even though our bodies die, because we are made in God's image we have a soul that lives forever. As sinners, we would live forever separated from God — but God had a plan to rescue us.

You see, as descendants of Adam and Eve, **each of us is born a sinner** (Romans 3:23). If we're honest with ourselves, we have to admit that each of us would have done the same thing Adam did, wouldn't we? In fact, every day, each of us disobeys the Creator's commands (Romans 5:12). We are probably much worse in our sin than Adam was! He lived 930 years and has one sin on record and we probably break that before breakfast! *(Yeah, God even knows what we are thinking!)*

For example, we may have told a lie (God says, "Do not lie"), disobeyed our parents (God says, "Obey your parents"), or said something unkind to a friend (God says, "Be kind to one another"). But even more, we were in Adam when he sinned! For example . . . where did your life come from? Your parents. Where did their life come from . . . their parents and so on back to Adam. When Adam sinned . . . we were there, too. Since we all sin, we are all under God's punishment for sin — death (Romans 6:23). We inherit Adam's nature — we are his descendants after all.

That's a lot of bad news, isn't it? **The good news is that God has lovingly given us a way of salvation from sin.** The Apostle Paul wrote: "For since by a man came death, by man also came the resurrection of the dead. For as in Adam all die, even so in Christ all shall be made alive" (1 Corinthians 15:21–22). God's Son stepped into history to become the "God-man." He became a perfect man — one of our relatives. Yes, He was of "one flesh" with us! He became our relative, so He, as a perfect man (but God at the same time) could pay the penalty for our sin and so provide a way for us to live with Him in heaven forever.

Since we all share a part in what Adam did and continue to sin against God as individuals, we need to humbly ask for forgiveness from our Creator. He is gracious and loving, and when we repent of our sin and believe Jesus died on the Cross in our place, **He gives us the free gift of eternal life with the Creator in heaven!**

Q7 If God really loved the world, why would He make a flood to

KILL EVERYONE OFF?

Bodie Hodge

God's beautiful and perfect world (Genesis 1) didn't stay good for long. After a short while, Adam disobeyed God's command (Genesis 3:6), and this sin brought a Curse on all of the creation. **God punished Adam's sin as He had said He would: with death** (Genesis 3:19).

Everyone born from that time on disobeys God (sins) and is under the same penalty of death that Adam was (Romans 3:23, 6:23). And just like Adam, people continued to sin. Sadly, during the time of a man named Noah, the whole population (except Noah and his family) had rejected God and behaved wickedly.

ADAM'S CHILDREN

Let's go back to the beginning. Check out Genesis 5. This chapter lists the men in the line from Adam until the Flood. *Math quiz:* Can you add the ages given in this chapter and figure out how many years passed from the time of Adam until the time of Noah? (For example, Adam was 130 years when Seth was born; Seth was 105 when Enosh was born . . . it's okay to use something to help you add it all up if you want!)

Answer: About 1,656 years. And during that time, men and women were having children. And each person born was a sinner. In fact, it got to the point the wickedness of man was so great that every thought was evil all the time, and the earth was filled with violence (Genesis 6:5 and 6:13). (Think about that — almost no one was thinking anything but bad stuff! That's as bad as it could get!)

God is sad when people sin because of His love for us. But sin separates us from God because He is holy (He is without sin). And because He is holy, anyone with sin cannot be with Him, and He must punish sin. By this time in history, God said He would punish the wickedness of mankind by sending a Flood that would cover the earth (Genesis 6). (Sort of like when you tried to do that big term paper and it was such a mess you tossed it to start over.)

But God showed His love by sending a means of salvation. He said He would save Noah and his family because Noah was obedient to God and lived by God's rules in righteousness. He gave Noah instructions about how to build an ark (a great ship) that would save his family and the land animal kinds from the Flood. During the time when Noah was working on the ark, he preached to the people around them (2 Peter 2:5). The people had plenty of time to turn from their sin (repent) and obey God. But they didn't. The ark was built large enough to save many people as well as the representatives of land-dwelling, air-breathing animals (Genesis 7:21–23). But people refused to listen.

Finally God caused the "springs of the great deep" to burst forth, cracking the earth's surface and sent rain on the earth. Water poured from above and below the earth's surface. The ark floated on the surface of the waters. The entire earth was covered with water and the Flood continued and all those who weren't on the ark died (Genesis 7). Noah, his family, and the animals on the ark made it safely through the year-long Flood. God created a new chance for mankind to obey His rules.

At the end of the Flood, God said the rainbow would be a reminder that He will never again judge the earth with such a watery catastrophe. **We've seen lots of local floods since** — but we've never seen (and will never see) a global Flood like that in Noah's day.

46

REMINDERS OF THE FLOOD

We also see reminders of the Flood in the many rock layers and fossils that formed as a result of the floodwaters mixing with lots of different types of mud and sand. Most of the fossil record is the graveyard of the Flood of Noah's day. When we see these rocks and fossils, we can remember that God isn't pleased with sin and must punish it.

But when we see a rainbow, we can remember God's loving promise that He will never again flood the entire earth for disobeying Him (Genesis 9). The Bible also tells us there will be another global Judgment — but next time by fire (2 Peter 3:7). God has provided an "ark of salvation" for us — the Lord Jesus Christ. He is our ark of salvation. Jesus said: "I am the door. If anyone enters by Me, he will be saved" (John 10:9).

God was patient in Noah's day — and God is patient with us today. "But, beloved, do not forget this one thing, that with the Lord one day is as a thousand years, and a thousand years as one day. The Lord is not slack concerning His promise, as some count slackness, but is longsuffering toward us, not willing that any should perish but that all should come to repentance" (2 Peter 3:8–9).

I pray every one of you can say you are in the ark of salvation.

"that if you confess with your mouth the Lord Jesus and believe in your heart that God has raised Him from the dead, you will be saved"
(Romans 10:9).

COMMANDED

BROUGHT

WATERED

RIVER

CREATED

RIVERHEA

GROUND

GIHON

WOMAN

EDEN

EVIL

DIE

COMPARABLE

PLANTED

GOOD

GOOD

FORMED

FATHER

How could God populate the world
with just two people

A FEW THOUSAND YEARS AGO?

Bodie Hodge

The Bible teaches that God created only two people in the beginning — Adam and Eve. And, from carefully studying the Bible, we know that "the beginning" was about 6,000 years ago according to the genealogies (those lists with all the "begat" words). The world's population today is estimated at almost 7 billion people. **Is 6,000 years enough time to produce all those people?**

IS IT REASONABLE?

The answer is absolutely! Scientists have estimated that the world's population doubles every 40 years (even taking into account death from diseases, famines, and natural disasters) — at least that has been the rate in recent times. Since we can't be sure of the rate in the past, let's be even more conservative. Let's say that the population doubles every 150 years. After 32 doublings (4,800 years), the world population would be about 8.6 billion people. From the time of Adam and Eve until a little after the time Jesus came to earth, the population should have reached more than 8 billion people by this calculation, so 6 to 7 billion is definitely possible.

However, that's not the entire story. We know that about 4,500 years ago (~2500 BC), a worldwide Flood wiped out the entire population of the world, leaving only eight people alive (Genesis 6–9; 1 Peter 3:20). Even so, as we can see with the calculations above, 4,500 years is pretty close to getting the population we have today, even with conservative estimates! (Yeah, even math provides a good confirmation of the Bible — cool, huh?)

WHERE ARE ALL THE PEOPLE?

Well now . . . let's look at this question from another perspective. Some people claim that the earth is billions of years old and that humans have been around for hundreds of thousands of years. If this were true, how large would we expect the world population to be?

Let's say that humans have been around for just 50,000 years. If we use the calculations above (one doubling every 150 years), there would have been 332 doublings! This means that the world's population would be almost unthinkable — a 1 followed by 100 zeros.

10,000,000,000,000,000,000,000,000,000,000,000,000,000,000,000,000,000,00

Clearly, this can't be correct and those who claim such long ages are wrong. In fact, even with death and war and disease knocking off people, we could still ask them the question, "Where are all the people?" And where are all the skeletons of the people who died?

AND THE ANSWER IS . . .

From a biblical perspective, we know that the earth (and universe) is about 6,000 years old. Of course, there was the bottleneck with the Flood where the population had to "start over."

Simple mathematical calculations from the population of the Flood until today give a great estimate that the human population should be around what we have — at least in the ball park anyway. Just do the math! But with the long age scenario, the numbers are outrageous . . . and simply wrong! That is unless they want to invoke a global catastrophe like a Flood to reduce the entire population . . . oh wait . . . that comes from the Bible.

00,000,000,000,000,000,000,000,000,000,000,000,000 *(that's a lot of zeros!)*

Q9 Should people from different races marry each other, or

IS THAT WRONG?

Dr. Tommy Mitchell

We know the Bible tells us how God created Adam (1 Corinthians 15:45) and that Eve was made from Adam's side, becoming the first woman (Genesis 3:20). So we know that all people everywhere have descended from these first two parents. **That means there's really only one race of people biologically — the human race!** We have two races of people spiritually though — those who have trusted in God for salvation and those who have not!

So why do people have different skin colors and speak different languages? After Noah and his family came off the ark, God told them to spread out and fill the earth. But Noah's descendants disobeyed that command. (Yep — more disobedience. Sin was happening again!) They built a tall tower they hoped would help keep them together. So God caused them to scatter over the earth by confusing their language (Genesis 11). Imagine everyone talking at once and only being able to understand your own family.

Babble Rabble

Over time these groups of people became isolated from one another. After all, they couldn't understand each other anymore because they did not speak the same language. **Each group eventually developed their own set of customs and habits.** Also, because they did not generally reproduce with others from outside their own language group, certain physical characteristics (traits some have referred to as "racial" characteristics — but they are only minor surface differences reflecting the great variability God put in our genes) became prominent in each group. Things like hair color, shapes of eyelids, and depth of skin tone (all humans are the same brown color — just different shades) eventually became quite different among the many people groups on the earth. However, all people are of one biological race. They are all of "one blood" (Acts 17:26).

Many people over the last 150 years have proposed that modern humans are the evolutionary descendants of an ape-like creature. Based on this mistaken idea, they have then believed that humans are of different "races," and that some "races" are more evolved than others.

After all, all these different so-called "races" could not have evolved to the same level at the same time, could they? This thinking has been shown to be very wrong — and sadly it has even fueled racism and prejudice. In recent years, scientists working on the Human Genome Project (they were studying human DNA) found that the difference between people groups is very small. Their results confirm that we're all one race biologically!

So it might be better to not even use the word "race" when taking about people. It would be much better to say that people are from a different "culture" or are from a different "ethnic" background. I prefer to say there are different "people groups." Even though we can easily see that people are different, we need to understand that the major differences are cultural — not racial as was once taught. It is most important to remember that all people are fully human.

Because we're all part of the human race, people from different tribes, countries, or nations are free to marry — there is no such thing as "interracial marriage" biologically. Actually, the Bible does speak against an "interracial marriage" — when two people from different "spiritual races" marry. In other words, the "interracial marriage" the Bible speaks against is when a Christian knowingly marries a non-Christian. You see, the Bible does give certain rules about marriage.

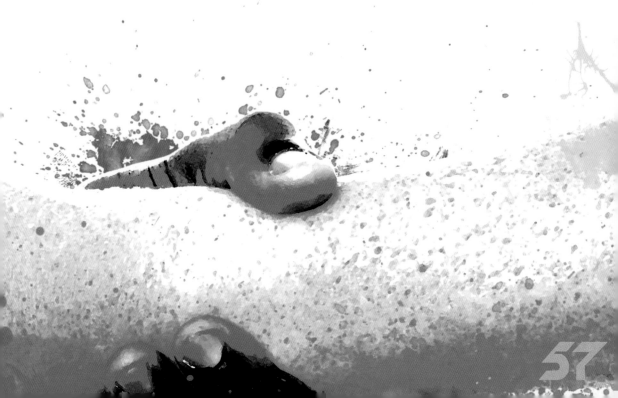

57

LOVE AND MARRIAGE

God established in the beginning that marriage would be between one man and one woman for life:

"And Adam said: 'This is now bone of my bones and flesh of my flesh; She shall be called Woman, because she was taken out of Man.' Therefore a man shall leave his father and mother and be joined to his wife, and they shall become one flesh" (Genesis 2:23–24). Jesus quoted from this passage in Matthew 19 when He answered a question about marriage.

And God makes it very clear that His children (Christians) should marry someone who is a Christian. In the Bible, the Apostle Paul tells us:

"Do not be unequally yoked together with unbelievers. For what fellowship has righteousness with lawlessness? And what communion has light with darkness?" (2 Corinthians 6:14). Here Paul is talking about the two "spiritual races."

You are probably laughing at the word "yoked," but seriously, it means being matched and put together with someone for life. This also applies to those we claim as close friends. Although Christians are to be witnesses to non-Christians (we live in this world — and are commanded to take the gospel message to everyone), we need to be careful about who we fellowship with closely. "Do not be deceived: 'Evil company corrupts good habits' " (1 Corinthians 15:33).

God is more concerned about what we look like spiritually (on the inside) than what we look like physically (on the outside). When the prophet Samuel went to anoint a new king of Israel, the Lord said to him:

> Do not look at his appearance or at his physical stature, because I have refused him. For the LORD does not see as man sees; for man looks at the outward appearance, but the LORD looks at the heart (I Samuel 16:7).

When we think about who we would like to marry, we need to be sure that we're following God's commands about a marriage partner. **Although it's easy to become attracted to a person based on outward appearances, we need to remember that a person's spiritual condition on the inside is what really matters.**

So — although we understand there is only one race biologically, there are two races spiritually! I pray you are in the right "spiritual race" — those who have received the free gift of salvation.

Q10 Why should I listen to what the

BIBLE SAYS ABOUT SEX?

Bodie Hodge

Life can be tough as a teenager, can't it? It was for me, and it was for the teens I have worked with. So my guess is that you are struggling as well — probably with a host of issues. One particular subject that seems to plague many teens nowadays is sex. (Yes, the Bible even has answers about that!)

SEX AND STANDARDS

It is a tough topic, and because it is, many church leaders, particularly youth pastors, avoid this topic like the plague! But let's face it: sex is an issue that needs to be addressed. Many may not know what God's Word says on this subject. So they need answers.

The secularists in today's society often push an agenda for an "anything goes" approach to sex, which includes orgies (open sex), teen sex, homosexual behavior, and other sexually "immoral" and adulterous actions, as well as sex on TV, movies, and in books. And they think it is okay, because they view people as animals with no moral standards. So they encourage young people to do whatever they want to do without regard for right or wrong.

But we as Christians have a higher standard (a higher authority) than that of others. We recognize that we are made in the image of God and are not mere animals. Because God made us, He gets to set the standard of morality. And that is a good thing!

Because God's very nature is good (Psalm 118:1), He tells us what is good (and bad) and how we should act. He gives us an absolute standard of morality, a set of principles that tell us how we should behave for our own well-being. In the Bible, His written Word to us, **He has told us what is right and what is wrong.**

Apart from God and His Word, there is no logical basis to distinguish between good and bad or right and wrong. In an atheistic, evolutionary worldview, people are merely chemicals reacting with each other. Would you be mad at titanium for reacting with carbon? If one set of chemicals decided to kill another set of chemicals, there is no logical reason to label murder as "wrong." Or if one set of chemicals decided to take something that didn't belong to it from another set of chemicals, there is no logical reason to label stealing as "wrong." These behaviors would simply be the results of chemical reactions — like mixing baking soda with vinegar. And life would be pretty miserable! From an atheistic, evolutionary perspective, you are really just a bag of chemicals!

However, because God is the Creator, you are not just a bag of chemicals. You are made in His image. You are special. In fact, so special that even though we rebelled against God in Adam (the first man), God paid the penalty for our sin. Wow, that is love! God values us that much. Because God is the Creator, He sets the rules (not to murder, rape, steal, lie, etc.). He loves us and wants us to be like Him. He knows what is best for us. He never changes and neither does His Word (Malachi 3:6; Psalm 119:89; Hebrews 13:8).

THE GIFT OF SEX

The Bible states that orgies are wrong (Romans 13:13), as are homosexual acts (1 Timothy 1:10), and the other sexually immoral things we've previously listed (1 Corinthians 6:9; Leviticus 18:23). Does this mean all sex is bad? Not at all! God created sex as a good thing — when it is done according to His purposes.

When God created Adam and Eve, He also blessed them. With them, He established the first marriage and defined marriage as being between one man and one woman (Genesis 2:20–25). Jesus affirmed this in Matthew 19 and Mark 10. He told them to have children (Genesis 1:28). And He declared it all "very good" (Genesis 1:31). This was the first family — the first and most fundamental of all human Institutions that God ordained.

In His original design, the Creator planned for sexual activity to be a good thing between husband and wife (God created marriage to be between one man and one woman for life). And it still is (Hebrews 13:4). In fact, an entire book of the Bible (the Song of Solomon) is devoted to showing the beautiful intimacy a husband and wife can share. (Yep, that's really in the Bible too!)

But after Adam sinned, people began to use sex in ways that went against God's rules and plans for mankind. Throughout the Old and New Testaments, God reminded His people that in order to be holy like He is, they must follow His commands. And one of the commands He continually gave concerned the proper place for sex. He forbids adultery (sex with someone other than your marriage partner (Exodus 20:14; 1 Corinthians 7) and fornication (sex before or outside of marriage; Ephesians 5:3; Colossians 3:5).

When we follow God's design for sex, we won't typically need to worry about contracting sexually transmitted diseases or becoming pregnant outside of marriage. **There is life in health in following God's loving instructions.**

Now I also know that in this sin-cursed world, there have been many issues that have disrupted the family. However, we must always try to the best of our ability, in the circumstances we are in, to ensure we obey what God has commanded us to do. And when we have done wrong, and come in true repentance, God is a forgiving God. And even though God does forgive us, sadly, we still have to live with the consequences of our sin — but we can trust in a gracious God to help us in our circumstances.

FOR TEENS WHO MAY HAVE MESSED UP . . .

- Don't give up. I once heard that just because you may have taken a million steps away from God (even regarding sex), it is only one step back. God is merciful and wants us to turn away from our sin. We should be humble and sorry for violating God's commands about sex, keeping in mind that one sin is worthy to be punished. And when we do repent, God forgives us. It is better to repent now than say, "Maybe one day I will." And the more we sin, the more negative consequences we will have to deal with and the more difficult it will be to turn away from those sins.

  If you find yourself in trouble, pregnant and scared about the consequences, please remember that God can take any bad situation and turn it into something good. Don't be pressured to take what the world says is a quick solution. Every life is precious, born and unborn, and abortion will profoundly impact your life in the future in ways you cannot even imagine.

  We want to encourage you to have a proper perspective on this subject. Instead of asking, "How intimate should I get with my boyfriend or girlfriend

before it is sinful?" ask **"How pure can I remain until I get married?"** Many people try to walk a fine line and are flirting with disaster, but that is not the way to go. We need to set apart Christ as Lord and let Him be the focus, in every relationship.

Times may change, but God's standards for morality, given in the Bible, are absolute and eternal. God loves those who obey His commands and He is pleased when we seek to follow Him. We can show our love for our Creator by joyfully obeying His Word.

Dr. Tommy Mitchell

Q11 If Christians are supposed to love everybody, why do they always seem to hate

GAY PEOPLE?

The issue of homosexuality is becoming more and more prominent in our culture. We see it discussed on the news. We see it openly displayed on TV shows and in movies. It is promoted in popular music, art, and in many of the books we read. It is so much an issue in society today that it becomes easy to wonder, **"What's the problem with homosexuality?"**

After all, if two people love each other, why shouldn't they be able to get married? So what if we are talking about two men or two women. Does it make a difference?

Well, it sure seems to matter to some folks. There are some who protest loudly against homosexual behavior. Some even call them names and make signs. They write letters to newspapers. They call in to radio shows. Some seem to shout loudly about how horrible homosexuals are.

But Christians are supposed to love everybody, aren't they? Can't Christians just accept homosexuals? Christians do accept homosexuals, but not homosexuality. Remember, hate the sin, not the sinner (Psalm 97:10). Even some who call themselves Christians say some nasty things about homosexuals.

In this case, the problem is the same on both sides of the issue. **The problem is sin.** There are people who hate the fact that the Bible shows homosexuality as a sin.

WHY IS THIS IMPORTANT?

God invented marriage. Genesis 2:18–25 explains that marriage is to unite one man and one woman. Jesus confirmed this definition in Matthew 19:4–6. So Scripture is clear about what God intended marriage to be — one man for one woman (a male and female).

Furthermore, the only rightful place for sex is within the bonds of marriage — one man and one woman. Any type of sexual behavior outside of such a marriage is sinful. Fornication (sexual activity between an unmarried man and woman) is also evil (1 Corinthians 6:9-10).

God is our Creator. He loves us and cares for us. Because He is God, He knows what is best for us. In His Word we learn how we should live our lives. By following His direction we can enjoy life to the fullest. So we should obey His instruction regarding marriage and sex.

Is Homosexual Behavior Wrong? Who Says?

Just as God's Word indicates that sex between an unmarried man and woman is sin, it indicates homosexuality is wrong. Romans 1:26–27 tells us, "For this reason God gave them up to vile passions. For even their women exchanged the natural use for what is against nature. Likewise also the men, leaving the natural use of the woman, burned in their lust for one another, men with men committing what is shameful, and receiving in themselves the penalty of their error which was due." Other verses dealing with this include Leviticus 18:22 and 1 Timothy 1:9–10.

Homosexual behavior is vile according to the Word of God. It is contrary to His plan for marriage, and it is a form of sexual sin. It is a sin that destroys the family that God instituted when he made the first man and first woman and commanded them to be "fruitful and multiply." And the family is God's unit to transmit His knowledge from one generation to the next and the world around.

Why Do Some People (Including Even Some Christians) Seem to Hate Gays?

Sadly, there are some who say they are Christians who do respond poorly when confronted with the issue of homosexuality. Their behavior is not fitting for those who call themselves children of the King. Their manner is like many non-Christians: being hateful and aggressive. And it must grieve the heart of our Lord.

We must remember that we are all born with a sinful nature. And we all have certain sins that we struggle with more than others. Some may have problems with lying, others with stealing, and others with sexual desires apart from marriage. Some may have a weakness in the area of homosexuality. Every person on this earth is a fallen, sinful creature. "And all our righteousnesses are like filthy rags" (Isaiah 64:6). But God also tells us there is no temptation we cannot overcome in Him. "No temptation has overtaken you except such as is common to man; but God is faithful, who will not allow you to be tempted beyond what you are able, but with the temptation will also make the way of escape, that you may be able to bear it" (1 Corinthians 10:13).

God's Word doesn't pretend that evil behavior is just another acceptable way to live. **As Christians, we should also take a stand on the Word and call sin what it is — sin.** This is true whether it be homosexuality, fornication, blasphemy, stealing, lying, idolatry, or even having an attitude of hatred toward another person. God holds us responsible for our actions.

We all know people who are genuinely hateful or belligerent. God does not condone (approve of) persecution of others, even by Christians. However, in today's world people are commonly accused of being "hateful" whenever they disagree with someone's lifestyle or dare to call anything wrong. Merely pointing out sinful behavior can often result in you being labeled a "hater." By this standard those who disagree with Christians could be called "haters," too, so this is not the proper way to think. We must always search our hearts and make sure we are not projecting hatred or contempt for other people when presenting God's truth.

Bible-believing, obedient Christians don't hate homosexuals. They merely wish them to repent and turn from their sinful ways. It is not the person that is hated, but the sin — the willful rebellion against God's Word. The good news is that God offers forgiveness for sin and has promised to help us overcome our struggles. Our job as Christians is to tell people that they need Jesus Christ and help them understand their need for the salvation and restoration He offers. The most loving thing we can do for someone is to lead him or her to Jesus.

"Let him know that he who turns a sinner from the error of his way will save a soul from death and cover a multitude of sins" (James 5:20).

Even though it may seem as if the majority around us think that homosexual behavior is okay, we can remember what God teaches us through His Word. And we can gently and lovingly share His truth with others.

"Let God be true but every man a liar"
(Romans 3:4).

71

Q12

How are we supposed to talk about God and the Bible in school when

IT'S ILLEGAL?

Bodie Hodge

First off . . . it is not illegal. Whoever says that is 100 percent wrong!

In the United States, the First Amendment to the Constitution states, **"Congress shall make no law respecting an establishment of religion"** and then states "or prohibiting the free exercise thereof." In other words, we have religious freedom (as long as it doesn't violate other governmental laws like murder, etc.) — the freedom to worship as we see fit. (See, that U.S. history class wasn't a waste of time, after all!)

This even applies to public schools. In 1990, the U.S. Supreme Court ruled that if a public school prohibited religious speech or activities, then it would be demonstrating hostility toward religion and would be unconstitutional (*Board of Education of the Westside Community Schools* vs. *Mergens, 496 US 226*). Many recent rulings by the court and laws established by Congress have given religious freedoms to public school students.

Students' Rights

Here are some examples to think about as you wonder whether a particular activity would be wrong at school.

- A student may wear a T-shirt or use a pencil with a religious message, Bible verse, or Christian slogan printed on it (i.e., if a student can wear a Judas Priest shirt, they can wear a Jesus shirt).

- Christian students are also able to pass out gospel tracts to classmates during non-instructional time in the same way that they are allowed to pass out non-religious materials. This should be done in a way that doesn't disrupt the normal events of a school day (i.e., if a student can pass out a flyer for a birthday party, he or she can pass out a tract about creation).

- Students can discuss religious matters or pray at any time when they are permitted to interact with other students — before and after school, during lunch, between classes — as long as the discussions don't constitute harassment of a particular person or group. Any time a student is permitted to discuss non-instructional matters, he may also discuss religious matters, which includes witnessing to and praying with others (i.e., if it is okay to talk about football, it is okay to talk about Christ).

- Prayer is protected under the first amendment. A student may pray before eating lunch or silently before taking a test . . . as long as there are tests, there will be prayer in school!

- Christians are able to read the Bible in school whenever other non-instructional books are permitted to be read — at lunch or during study hall, for example (i.e., if students can read a vampire novel, then students can read the Bible).

- Students may express their religious beliefs in any written or oral assignment. If the views of all other students are allowed, the teacher may permit a Christian to share his views, as well (i.e., if it is okay to profess one's views about PETA, then it is okay to profess one's views about Jesus or creation).

- Public secondary schools must give Bible clubs the same privileges as any other school club, as long as the club is led by a student and not by a faculty sponsor. Bible club meetings may include prayer, Bible reading, and singing (i.e., if it is okay to have a book club, then it is okay to have a Bible club).

- Christian students may be excused from a lesson or activity which would "substantially burden a student's free exercise of religion, and if the school cannot prove a compelling interest in requiring attendance, the school is legally required to excuse the student from that lesson or activity." (Don't let a teacher make you violate your conscience.)

The underlying principle of all of these guidelines is that the student must not disrupt classroom or school order. As you can see, it is not illegal to talk about God or the Bible in public school. The more you know your rights as a public school student, the more you're able to exercise those rights in witnessing to non-Christians and fellowshiping with other believers.

WHAT ABOUT TEACHERS?

Teachers in a public school do not have the same rights as students since they represent the state. They are not supposed to affirm a particular religion. Even so, many teachers teach the religion of secular humanism openly (evolution, millions of years, big bang, no God, etc.). Perhaps one day, that religion can also be removed from the classroom, but right now the state allows that religion to be promoted by teachers and textbooks. Some states still permit teachers to question the religion of secular humanism.

Many teachers are Christians, and we want to encourage them. **We all need to be praying for them.** Some teachers offer an after school optional class to discuss problems with the religion of secular humanism or how observational science is a good confirmation of the Bible (problems with evolution, millions of years, origin of life, big bang, etc.). But since they are not usually permitted to do this during school hours, they have to do it in other ways.

Conclusion

Students and teachers have different rights in public/state schools. As a student in a public/state school you have a lot of rights, but remember many of your teachers are limited.

Keep in mind that in college it is more likely the other way around. Professors have "academic freedom," especially when they have tenure (can't be fired), so they can attack or promote any religion they want. Sadly, many openly attack Christianity. But students in college, though you have the freedoms to pray or witness, must be careful. Many teachers may fail you if they find out you are Christian, or make it very difficult for you to graduate. These are just some thoughts to consider if you go to a secular college. You may want to stick with a college that believes in biblical authority. See **www.answersingenesis.org/colleges/**.

How can we be sure Jesus is the

ONLY WAY TO GET TO GOD ?

Bodie Hodge

You may hear from your friends or read in books that there are many ways to God. "It doesn't really matter what you believe as long as you believe something." It's easy to be confused about the truth about how we get to heaven.

But the fact is, there is only one God and He is the only one qualified to inform us how to bridge the gap that separates us from Him. Around 2,000 years ago, Jesus said He is the only way to God: "I am the way, the truth, and the life. No one comes to the Father except through Me" (John 14:6).

That's a pretty bold claim, isn't it? How do we know all other paths are wrong, and He really is the only way we can get to God?

Jesus (God's Son) was the only one to come from heaven to save us, not other religious leaders. The Bible says:

> For I have come down from heaven, not to do My own will, but the will of Him who sent Me. This is the will of the Father who sent Me, that of all He has given Me I should lose nothing, but should raise it up at the last day. And this is the will of Him who sent Me, that everyone who sees the Son and believes in Him may have everlasting life; and I will raise him up at the last day (John 6:38–40).

If Jesus were just a good man, as some people claim, we wouldn't have any reason to trust His claim to be the only way to heaven. In fact, some might think He was either lying or a little crazy. However, He showed while He was on earth that He really was who He claimed to be — so much more than just a good man: **He is the Son of God**, the second Person of the triune God. Jesus, who is the Creator (Colossians 1:16), became the God-man — truly man, but truly God! He became a perfect man — **without sin.**

ONLY JESUS . . .

Is perfect. He never sinned, never disobeyed God's commands (1 John 3:5). No other religious leader was perfect (Buddha, Confucius, Muhammad, Joseph Smith, etc.).

Completely forgives sins (Mark 2:1–12). When someone sins against us, we may be able to forgive him or her for that particular sin, but only Jesus offers forgiveness for all the sin someone has done in his or her life. No other person can take away the sin of the world.

Fulfilled many prophecies (Jeremiah 23:5; Matthew 2:1–2). The chances of Jesus fulfilling just eight prophecies given in the Old Testament is the same as if you stacked 100 trillion silver dollars in an area the size of Texas, two feet deep, marked one of them, threw it into the pile, blindfolded a man, and gave him one chance to find it. The chance that he'd pick the marked one on the first try is impossible — just like the chance that Jesus would fulfill eight prophecies. Yet the Old Testament makes over 60 major prophecies about Jesus' first coming to earth. And Jesus fulfilled them perfectly when He came to earth to become a man!

Heals sickness and disease (Luke 4:38–40). Jesus made the lame walk, the blind see, the deaf hear, and cured many from diseases! Who else can say they were able to do that in their own power?

Has power over nature (Luke 8:22–25). Jesus showed His incredible power when He commanded the winds and waves to be still, and they obeyed! Since He is the Creator, He has power over His creation (John 1:1–5; Colossians 1:16)!

Has power over death (Luke 7:11–17). Jesus raised many people from the dead! And He even raised Himself from the dead (John 10:17–18) — see the next point for more on this!

Rose from the dead (Matthew 27–28). Perhaps the biggest evidence that Jesus is who He claimed to be is His Resurrection. No other person, including all religious leaders, has ever risen from the dead and is still alive today! After His Resurrection, He was seen by many people (Acts 10:40) — over 500 at one time (1 Corinthians 15:6)!

Is God (John 1:1–3, 4:5–26; Colossians 1:14–17). Jesus claimed to be God, and you can see with all of the above that He is who He claimed to be. Only Jesus lived a life that backed up His claims.

Could take the punishment we deserve (Hebrews 2:9; Philippians 2:8). The punishment from an infinite God is an infinite punishment and just one sin is worthy of this punishment. God, being perfectly holy, has to punish sin. And the punishment for sin is death culminating in an eternal death in hell (Luke 12:5). Jesus Christ, the Son of God who is infinite, is the only One who could take the punishment from the infinite Father. This is why Jesus had to die. Only He could do it — we never could. But the wrath of God was satisfied when Jesus, who was sinless, became sin for us and died the death we deserve. But the power is in the Resurrection. In the same way Christ was resurrected, we are delivered from death through Christ (death has no sting 1 Corinthians 15:55–57).

Jesus Is the Only Way!

As we've seen in this book, the Bible is true and God cannot lie (Hebrews 6:18): we can trust Jesus when He says that He is the only way to heaven. All other ways are not true. When we read and study God's Word, we can know the truth about God and how we can spend eternity with Him in heaven.

Q14 The Bible...and

DINOSAURS... AND DRAGONS?

Ken Ham and Bodie Hodge

Often teens come home from school and ask their Christian parents about dinosaurs. If they were to search the Bible for answers, they would quickly find that the word "dinosaur" is not in the Bible! (Actually, that is because this word "dinosaur" wasn't even invented until 1841 — long after the Bible was translated into English!) At this point, many parents may give up, being unsure of what to say, but the Bible does have answers on this subject. (There are specific details on dinosaurs in it — but more about how to find that later!)

Dinosaurs were land animals. We'll exclude flying reptiles and sea creatures, because, by definition, dinosaurs were land animals, with their legs directly under their body. This is why crocodiles, komodo dragons, etc., are not considered dinosaurs. On what day did God create land animals? The Bible says it was on day 6 (Genesis 1:24–31). **So dinosaurs along with other animals were made on day 6**, the same day as the first man and woman. Remember a perfect, all-knowing God who has always been there would know.

It All Adds Up

Now if you add up the years in the genealogies from Adam to Abraham, and then add the years from the birth of Christ to the present day, this adds up total of about 6,000 years. So instead of dinosaurs living and dying out millions of years before man existed, they were actually created about 6,000 years ago along with the first humans. You can trust a perfect God's Word over imperfect man's ideas about the past, such as millions of years (which is just a popular guess by atheists and secular scientists that hasn't been proven). So no matter how many times people say that dinosaurs lived millions of years ago, that doesn't make what they say true. **A lie or a bad guess can be repeated many times, but it doesn't prove that is what really happened.**

So the dinosaurs are not that old! Bet you also didn't know that dinosaurs were originally vegetarian (Genesis 1:30). (Even big old T-Rex!) But something changed. When Adam sinned, the world was drastically altered (Genesis 3). That's why T-Rex went from munching plants to chomping prey!

Fast forward almost 1,700 years and the world was pretty much a cesspool of sin (Genesis 6:5). God had enough, and decided to judge the world's wickedness with a global Flood. You know the account in the Bible from there. One righteous man, Noah, built a huge ark with three decks (so long you could have played a real football game on it and not reached the ends). God told Noah to bring a pair of every land-dwelling, air-breathing animal aboard the ark (seven of some) (Genesis 7:2–3). This would have included dinosaurs! With around 50 known dinosaur "created kinds" (or families), there would have been a variety of these creatures on Noah's ark.

Dinosaurs that were not aboard Noah's ark died. Some probably decayed, but many were buried rapidly with sediment from the Flood and fossilized. In fact, we find quite a few dinosaur fossils in fossil layers deposited by the Flood in different parts of the world today. Now since the Flood was just under 4,500 years ago — most fossils are only about that old!

WHAT ABOUT THE BIG DINOSAURS? NO WAY THERE WAS ROOM . . . OR WAS THERE?

Even the largest dinosaurs were once smaller when they were young. In fact, most dinosaurs were small, with an average size nearly that of a sheep. The largest dinosaur eggs we find are just slightly larger than a football. So when it came to the biggest dinosaurs like Sauropods, it makes more sense for Noah to take the young adults on the ark — less food, less waste, and less space. However, there was plenty of room regardless. (Oh, and creationists believe a huge Sauropod could be a creature mentioned in the Bible. Behemoth in Job 40:15 — read not only how impressive this creature was, but that it was described by a man who actually had his encounter with this great animal recorded. Lucky for us, he wasn't limited to a tweet-sized description in order to share what he saw!)

Just A Dinosaur by Another Name

There came a time when very few dinosaurs were around and people began telling of their encounters with rare reptilian serpents that they didn't see anymore. Then the stories became embellished and distorted — leading to what are known as dragon legends. Many of the descriptions of the dragons in these encounters are most likely just references to what we call today "dinosaurs."

So many of the old dragon legends and accounts may well go back to an actual encounter with a dinosaur before they died out. Recall the legends of St. George killing the dragon, the Gilgamesh epic records a dragon being slain, and China has many stories of dragons and dragon images. (But there are many other dragon legends from every continent of the world!) **A number of old books recount events that occurred with dragons.** Some may even be in your school or church library!

By the 1800s people began taking a closer look at fossils that people had been finding for thousands of years — some referred to them as "dragon bones." In reality, they were re-discovering a group of creatures created on day 6 by God — dinosaurs!

In 1841, a British scientist, Sir Richard Owen, invented the word dinosaur. Since the King James Bible was first translated into English in 1611, you won't find the word "dinosaur" in this Bible or those versions that came from this translation!

There's really no big mystery surrounding dinosaurs; they were created on day 6 alongside Adam and Eve. Sin affected the world. The Flood affected the world. Many of those that didn't go on Noah's ark were fossilized — being buried during the Flood. Like lots of other animals, dinosaurs have become extinct since the Flood — but they lived up until relatively recent times (thus the dragon legends).

"As for God, His way is perfect; the word of the LORD is proven. He is a shield to all who trust in Him" (2 Samuel 22:31).

Why would God ever want to save someone as

MESSED UP AS ME?

Dr. Tommy Mitchell

We all do things that we know are wrong, don't we? We disobey our parents, take something that doesn't belong to us, tell a lie, really want cool things other people have that don't belong to us, say hurtful and unkind things, lose our temper when things don't go our way . . . and the list goes on. **Frankly, we are all far from perfect. Very far.**

Romans 3:23 says, "For all have sinned and fall short of the glory of God." All means *all*. All of us sin. But knowing everybody else does too doesn't excuse what I do.

Discouraging, isn't it? Do you ever feel that you are just too far gone for God to care about? Have you messed up so badly that you're sure you've ruined your life? So badly you're sure even God has given up on you? (He hasn't) **You are not alone.** Really, you are not alone!

GOD IS PERFECT

God is perfect (Psalm 145:17; 1 John 1:5). God cannot sin. He desires that we all be as perfect as He is. He says, "Be holy, for I am holy" (1 Peter 1:16).

So there is the problem, isn't it? We are supposed to be holy, but we have all fallen short because we are sinners — we sinned in Adam. Even the best people fail to measure up when compared to God, as we are all descendants of Adam.

So how does this help? You're thinking, *I already know I'm messed up, and now you point out that I'm even worse than I thought, and everybody else is messed up too!*

When God created Adam, he was perfect. . . . God gave Adam a simple rule and a choice to obey. **But Adam wanted to do things his own way.** Adam did not like having to obey a rule, so he didn't. Adam fell short of God's standard of perfection. He fell short of God's glory. He was no longer perfect. He brought sin into the world. (But notice, things don't end there! God's love for us doesn't end either!)

Like our original parents, Adam and Eve, **each of us disobeys God's commands** (we inherit that sin nature from Adam). We all fall short of His standard of perfection. We're all in the same boat — from the vilest murderer to the sweetest old lady we know — we're all sinners. That's the bad news.

God Is Judge

God is holy and righteous. He cannot tolerate sin. Sin carries a penalty and must be punished. It has been so from the beginning of the world. Genesis tells us that God told Adam not to eat of the tree of the knowledge of good and evil. God made it clear that if he did so, he would die. Adam disobeyed God anyway. So Adam (and all of us, as we are descendants of Adam and have his nature) committed high treason against the Creator God. Thus, death and corruption entered this once-perfect world. The horrible penalty of sin is death (Romans 6:23).

God Is Redeemer

Even in His righteous judgment, God offered grace and mercy to those created in His image.

After Adam sinned, God provided Adam and Eve with clothing made from the skin of an animal (Genesis 3:21). That was the first time any animal died. Adam and Eve were probably very sad to see such a beautiful animal die. But sin was serious business, and its consequences are no laughing matter. When God made clothes of skin to cover their bodies and their shame, He wanted them to know He was also planning a way to completely take away their sin.

From that time on, people sacrificed animals to show God that they were sorry for their sin and that they knew they needed to have their sin covered by the blood of another. In doing so, they also understood they were looking forward to the ultimate sacrifice that would be once and for all. (That's why these sacrifices are not longer needed!) **God promised to send someone who would defeat Satan's plans to destroy all people**. God promised to send One who could pay the penalty for human sin and triumph over death (Genesis 3:15).

About 4,000 years after God made that promise, He sent His Son to earth to become the God-man. While on earth, Jesus did what Adam didn't do — lived a life of perfect obedience to God. And even though He never sinned and didn't deserve to die, He was put to death on the Cross. He let Himself be crucified because He loves us enough to take our punishment for us (Romans 5:8).

The most amazing news is that Jesus rose from the dead three days later!
God accepted His sacrifice on the Cross in payment for sin. Jesus made a way for us to spend eternity with God forever! When we say we are sorry for our sin (repent) and believe that Jesus died on the Cross in our place and rose from the dead, God gives us the gift of eternal life. The names of those who have received this gift are written in a special book called the Lamb's Book of Life. Do you know for certain that your name is written there?

"For God so loved the world that He gave His only begotten Son, that whoever believes in Him should not perish but have everlasting life" (John 3:16).

But I'm Too Messed Up!

Yeah, right. You think you're the only one who's ever been a total failure? Read the Bible — it's full of people who failed and God still used them for amazing things! Face it, God loves you — no matter what!

You think you're more messed up than Moses, who was a murderer? More messed up than David, who was both a murderer and an adulterer? More messed up than Paul? All he did was track down and persecute the early Christians. You think you're more messed up than these men?

Moses eventually led the Israelites out of captivity and received the Ten Commandments from God's own hand on Mount Sinai. David became a man after God's own heart (Acts 13:22). Paul became the greatest Christian missionary in history. How did that happen? Simply this, they put their faith and trust in God, received the free gift of salvation, and their lives were transformed.

No, they did not become sinless. They were still fully human, capable of failure at a moment's notice. Paul even wrote in the Bible (Romans 7: 15-24) that he got so frustrated with his own sinfulness that he felt wretched!

Moses, David, Paul — their sin still carried a penalty (for example, they all died physically). There are always consequences to our actions. But Moses and David and Paul did not have to pay the ultimate penalty, eternal separation from God (that's the eternal death the Bible talks about — hell). And neither do you. God also blessed them by giving them great things to do for Him and a very close personal relationship with Him.

So you are NOT too messed up. No one is. God desires that you repent, turn from your sins, and put your trust in Jesus Christ. You're not too broken for God to fix.

Why does God want to save sinful wretches like you and me? Because He loves each of us so much He wants us to spend eternity with Him in heaven! Sin and death have no place in heaven. So God made a way for us to come to heaven and leave sin behind forever. **He did that by sending Jesus to pay sin's price for us.** All He asks is that we repent and trust Him.

> And he brought them out and said, "Sirs, what must I do to be saved?"
> So they said, "Believe on the Lord Jesus Christ, and you will be saved, you and your household" (Acts 16:30–31).

"But God demonstrates His own love toward us, in that while we were still sinners, Christ died for us" (Romans 5:8).